Stories in the End

Stories in the End:

Short Letters from a Long Life

Jay Eldred

Tom Poole

Copyright © 2019 Jay P. Eldred

All rights reserved. This book or any portion thereof may not be reproduced or used in any manner whatsoever without the express written permission of the publisher except for the use of brief quotations in a book review.

Everything here is true, but may not be entirely factual. Parts have been fictionalized to varying degrees, for various purposes. In some cases, the authors could not remember the exact words said by certain people, and exact descriptions of certain things, and so had to fill in gaps as best they could. Otherwise, all characters and incidents and dialogue are real, and are not products of the authors' imaginations.

For Barbara

Friends that I loved, and still do love . . . tell them my song.

Richard II

Prelude

My Dear Friend,

In life you would have called me Thomas Judson Poole, or more simply, Mr. Tom. I was born August 28, 1918 and died February 3, 2017. I've heard it said life is the dash lived between the dates on your tombstone. This is my dash.

If you knew me in person, you might wonder why I didn't write all this sooner. Why I didn't tell more stories, crack more jokes, share more words of wisdom? I can't tell you, exactly, only that I did what seemed right to me at the time. And it's not quite true I didn't write anything; I wrote pages of stories – I just didn't share them.

Now, my story is finally being told with the help of my good friend Jay. In many ways we are – were? – two peas in a pod. Among other things, he's an old soul in a young body. For many years I was an old soul in an old body. We understood each other, we respected each other, and for nearly eleven years we called each other friend.

Jay teaches history, and being that sort of mind, several years ago asked about recording some of my stories as we sat around the kitchen table. I said no for two reasons: First, I get nervous around recording equipment. Second, stories tend to ramble. I thought I'd be wasting his time if I started out talking about one thing and ended up on something completely different. Thinking back, I might have done things differently, but it's too late to change it now.

Instead, I compromised with him: he could tell my story on two conditions. I didn't want to know if or when I was being recorded, and I made him promise to wait until after I was gone to write a single word.

I didn't tell him about the help I'd give. I began writing my own stories late at night, suffering the sleeplessness of the aged. I'd go into the kitchen, turn on the lamp, and write. I wrote about growing up, about serving in the Navy during the war, about the kinds of things that just seem to happen to a person over nearly a century.

I didn't tell him about the documents I saved: everything and anything that might be important. I wasn't a hoarder, though, keeping everything neatly filed and organized and ready for someone willing to read through them and put the pieces back together like a jigsaw puzzle. Someone like a historian. Receipts, forms, service records, brochures, some papers seemingly put in at random but all with a purpose – you just have to connect the dots.

This was my final gift to Jay: the sources needed to tell my story. The memories of sitting around the table, talking about anything and everything. The written record I left behind. The photographs stacked neatly in cardboard boxes. Not for him to own, but to use, to piece together a short history of me for those I left behind. For you, who I may have never met.

My family and friends will find some of these stories familiar, though they might remember them differently. Some stories will be brand new; still others you might not believe. But everything happened, more or less. These are – after all – *my* stories. The ones I told around the kitchen table

– sometimes even *about* the kitchen table – while watching the news or the ball games, while eating supper, or playing board games. They are the stories I wrote down and the stories I left to be discovered.

Though they are mine, I have left them for another to share. Like stories told around the campfire, they might not be exactly as you remember. Everyone has a different voice, a different perspective, a different way of thinking. So think of these stories for what they are: stories told as families gather and share stories of days gone by. No one remembers every detail, but detail isn't important. It's the telling of the story itself that's important. In telling the story, we feel as if those involved are still with us, as if they're not truly gone so long as we can remember them. We forget the sound of their voice, their smell, the things that made them *them* – yet they live on in our stories. In some small way, it gives us hope that one day, we, too will be remembered in someone else's story, if only to say "Did I ever tell you the story great-grandpa once told me about his great-grandpa?".

In stories we achieve a kind of immortality.

★ ★ ★

You know, they called my generation the "Greatest Generation". There are fewer and fewer of us every year; soon there will be no more. One day you will wake up and hear the news the last living World War II veteran has died. One day no one will remember Pearl Harbor or VE or VJ Day. No one could tell you where they were when President Kennedy was shot or how they saw man walk on the moon in grainy black and white. No one to share with first-hand experience the anguish of the *Challenger* explosion or the optimism of the Berlin Wall crashing down. One day, there will be those who do not remember 9/11; already high school seniors are graduating who were not born then.

I can tell you, and I can remember, because I was there. Now I am gone; you must remember for me.

I will estimate dates and ages as I'm not sure they are exact, but I've already attempted to write the basics of these stories in my own hand:

Railroad Tracks and Head Injury

Tree Climb Clark Ave.

Shotgun Scare

Bear Trap Scare

Bridge Dive - leg injury

Fall in Yellowstone Park

Navy (Pearl)

Cherbourg invasion (D-Day)

Sinking of #726

Trapping

Bullets through Cap

Rabbit Hunt - I Shot Eddie

Jay can fill in the details.

If you don't mind, I'll share these stories as if writing to my dear friend B.
It's comfortable to talk that way. Thank you for understanding.

- Mr. Tom

Selected

Homilies

Dear B.,

Where did you come from, where did you go?

Where did you come from, Cotton-Eye Joe?

Or so the old song goes.

I've seen the ads on TV: companies claiming to use your DNA to examine your genetics and tell you where you come from. I've watched those TV shows, too, where genealogists tell celebrities their family stories. You know, I remember a time when DNA wasn't even a thing, let alone advertized on television.

These folks are trying to substitute facts for stories. They tell you the countries you're supposedly from, and then their ads show pretty folks "discovering" their roots. Why did their family stories stop? I don't know, but I can't help but feel sorry for them.

Down here we don't talk about family as such, we talk about "our people". Your people and where they're from can tell you most anything you need to know about a person, whether they're from the Outer Banks or Harkers Island or Down the County as we like to say. My people come from all over Eastern North Carolina. I was born in Goldsboro, twenty-four years before the military started building Seymour Johnson Air Force Base. Two years later, my parents and I moved toward the coast, down to New Bern. That's me. That's my people. But my folks didn't hail from Goldsboro. My father, Thomas J. Poole, Sr. was born around 1891 or 1892 in Virginia. My mother, Mary Corbel Poole, was born in 1896 in the Outer Banks of North Carolina to a Mrs. Hollie Parker.

It's through my mother and grandmother that my family had its first brushes with fame. They lived in Currituck County, North Carolina - out on the Outer Banks. Long before the islands became the tourist destination they are today, the people of the Banks were fishermen and coastal farmers. The early 1900s found my mother and her family near Nags Head and Kill Devil Hills.

I'll wager you can tell where I'm going with this. My mother was at Kill Devil Hills in the fall of 1903 when those two Wright brothers from Ohio made history.

According to family legend, my mother and her mother watched the brothers as they worked on - and eventually flew - their *Wright Flyer*, watching them from the top of nearby dunes. I once saw (or thought I saw) a picture of Orville and Wilbur Wright, and in the background, shadowy figures just recognizable as people: a woman and a small girl - my mother and grandmother. I can't recall the last time I saw that photograph, and Jay's searching the National Archives has turned up nothing like what I saw.

I have to wonder if this is just exaggerated family history. Maybe it's a false memory combining different events from my childhood, or a story our family has told itself so long we believe it. After all, it's both possible and probable such a thing actually happened.

But if I'm remembering things incorrectly, what's the real story? Did they see the brothers but never showed up in photographs? Did they even see them at work at all? That they must have seen them in town seems beyond dispute, but what about the details?

Maybe the photograph is in a private collection somewhere, waiting to be found again and prove my family's claim to be an eyewitness to history.

Well, this bit of history at any rate. I've seen more than my fair share of historical events.

But if my memory is failing, what does that say about everything in these pages? If something can't be backed up by a paper document, did it really happen?

Well, I trust my memory because I work my mind. I watch Wheel of Fortune and can still solve the puzzles. I complete word searches, though for the last several years I've had to get them in large print. I write lists late at night: lists from memory of books of the Bible, of Presidents and Vice-

Presidents and the years they served, of states and their capitals, of United States currency and the people pictured on it.

The currency gives me problems, sometimes, especially when it comes to larger bills that have been out of circulation for some time or ones I haven't seen recently. For example, I can never remember who's on the $1000 bill. Obviously, it's President Grover Cleveland. Sure, I can remember it now, but I'm not making my list now. When I'm making the list, it'll be gone.

You know, I used to have a few of those bills, but not for quite some time. I'm pretty sure the dealer took me for a ride when he bought them from me, but that's just how things sometimes work out. No use complaining about things that can't be changed.

Speaking of claims to fame, though, I've had a few of my own. Most of them I'll have to save for later - why tell you everything up front? Then you won't stick around, and I love company to eat with, to watch the game, to just sit and talk, or even to just sit as the mood strikes.

Anyhow, I've taken at least two celebrities hunting.

I went hunting with Babe Ruth on one of his trips down from New York. If I recall rightly, he favored duck hunting and would often take a boat and guide out of New Bern. This would have been in my teens. I've also had the golfer Arnold Palmer sit at my kitchen table. It's a shame I can't find any of the pictures from those visits.

How did we get on this track? Oh, that's right - our people, our family. Family is more than blood, you know. There's blood that doesn't always act like family and folk without a drop of related blood that's more than family could ever be. I reckon family are those folk there for you when there's nothing to get in return.

Back to my folks, though. They were married on May 5, 1915, in Goldsboro, North Carolina. It was there I was born three years later, and we moved to New Bern when I was three or so.

And now that I'm starting to repeat myself, I think that's enough for today.

Until next time.

Love,

Tom

Dear B.,

You once asked about my earliest memory. Maybe it was Jay or someone else entirely. Point is, I've been thinking about memories lately. I've racked up quite a few in my time, and at my age I can't always remember them all exactly. It's a good thing Amber took time to label all the photos in those cardboard boxes, eh? They can sometimes jog my memory back in the right direction.

It amazes me how often memory shows up on television. And I don't just mean on game shows like Jeopardy! or Wheel of Fortune, or on crime shows where some random bit of knowledge solves a tough case. Memory makes actual news, especially when some big anniversary is coming about:

Where were you when you found out President Kennedy had been shot?

Working at the plant.

Where were you when Challenger *exploded?*

Watching it live on T.V.

What were you doing on September 11?

Getting ready to head into the woods - with only a month or so left to the start of hunting season, I still had a few bucks to scout.

Of course, there's one question I get asked the most:

Where were you on December 7, 1941 - the day the Japanese attacked Pearl Harbor?

That particular answer is too long to tell here with the time I have right now. I'll have to sit down and write a letter or two just about that.

Someday.

It's funny, talking to Jay about memory. His earliest memory is watching the Berlin Wall come down. That was only what, '88 or '89? Seems like yesterday to me. Then again, most days feel like yesterday. They all run together in the end.

Where was I? Oh yes, memory. I was thinking about my earliest memory because of something Jay asked me some time ago. I reckon he was working on his senior college paper at the time, and he asked me if I knew anything about the Great New Bern Fire of 1922. Now, I was just a few months over four years old at the time, so I can't remember the details first-hand, you understand, but the facts of the matter are these:

On December 1, 1922, a fire started in a lumber mill near downtown New Bern. Some say a second fire started in someone's house at the same time. Well, anyway, it was a big fire made worse by the fact it was an extremely windy day and embers kept being blown all over the place. Add to that the fact many firemen and volunteers who would've worked to put out the fire were out of town cheering on the high school football team to a state championship victory in Raleigh. A good portion of downtown burned; in fact, some people say the walls of Cedar Grove Cemetery are still black from the fire and smoke. That might be some of it, but those walls are also made of coral brick (or at least they were) and that stuff picks up everything under the sun.

They never did decide how the fire actually started. They arrested a bum and accused him of starting the fire in the lumber mill. He served time for it, but as I recall he was also deemed insane - what they call "mentally incompetent" today - probably guilty of nothing more than being in the wrong place at the wrong time.

Back to my memory. We lived over in Ghent at the time and my Daddy took me walking through the charred rubble. I remember walking with him, but I don't really remember what I saw. Instead, I remember the smell: it smelled like burned chicken feathers. It was an awful smell that got into everything, even our clothes, and Mama had to scrub extra hard to get those outfits clean again, and we hadn't even done anything in them but walk around. To this day I can't stand the smell of burned chicken. It simply turns my stomach.

I hope your first memory is more pleasant than mine.

Well, that's enough of a trip down memory lane for one day. I trust I've given you something to think over and talk about the next time we see each other.

Take care.

Love,

Tom

Dear B.,

I'm sitting outside on the back porch, watching the birds fight off the squirrels at the red bluebird feeder, and I just heard a train whistle. How many lines run through New Bern now? I suppose it depends on how you count. By my reckoning, there's three branches with the junction down on National Avenue: the track across the Neuse River, the track that heads through Sunnyside and Woodrow and on towards who knows where, and the track that runs through downtown by the library and the old New Bern Academy and the new Farmer's Market building before crossing the Trent River and running on down toward Bayboro and eventually Greenville or some such place.

If I can hear the train here, then it must be coming down that last track. I always wonder and worry about that one. Back in the day everyone knew when the train was coming. Unless you were deaf, you could hear the rumble and rattle and whistle long before you saw it coming down the rails. Nowadays everything's so insulated and closed up tight and people so distracted, it's a wonder more people don't get hit or their cars run over, especially down on Hancock Street where the cars are parked just about on the track! Of course, it still happens occasionally, but you don't hear about it much, do you?

One thing for certain about trains: if you've got to cross the tracks and you're in a hurry, the crossing guard will always be down. I'm preaching to the choir on this one, aren't I? You know what it's like to be headed here and come up on the junction and see the red lights flashing and the gates coming down. How many times have you tried to beat the train by taking the side road by the old Maola milk plant, only to see the train's crossing the river? Then, you're faced with a choice: sit and wait for who knows how long or backtrack all the way up National Avenue and Oaks Road to Glenburnie, and even then there's no guarantee. Some of those trains are monsters, and every once in a while one'll cut off that entire section of town at all three crossings. I always pray there's not a fire truck or ambulance that needs to get through.

Growing up, we kids were all taught not to play around the trains. Don't play on the tracks. Don't try to jump on or off the cars. Don't put pennies on the tracks. Folks said trains had been derailed by little kids putting their pocket change on the tracks, but I don't think that was right. I think folks just didn't want their kids wasting money. A penny went a long way back in the 20s, a lot farther than it does today, I can tell you that.

Of course, I didn't always listen. Imagine that: a kid who doesn't listen to his parents. Anyway, when I was eight or nine years old I took a serious fall while walking the railroad track, which at that time ran on Park Avenue through Ghent. I shouldn't have been walking there anyway, but I was, and the track was icy and I slipped, hit my head, and was knocked temporarily unconscious. I was carried to the hospital - this would be St. Luke's on the corner of Broad and George Streets - where the doctors determined I'd suffered a concussion. I ended up laid up sick in bed for several weeks as a result.

I suppose I've taken enough of your time for one afternoon, but I'll be sure to write again soon.

In the meantime, be safe.

And avoid the trains.

Love,

Tom

Dear B.,

You'll never guess what the neighbor's cat just did.

That silly Kelly climbed a tree here in the yard and then couldn't get herself down again. She cried and mewed until Ike and I came to her rescue.

And now I'm thinking about trees and cats, or cats and trees. I'm not sure the order. Let's talk about trees first.

There used to be trees everywhere around here, which made for decent hunting. Most of the shopping district in New Bern today was once prime hunting land for various animals; leastways, it was good enough for a couple of teenage boys to spend their days there. Of course, there're no trees there now except for those planted by the real estate developers.

And the streets - there used to be trees all along the streets, too. Oaks Road used to have oak trees. Now, there's what, a handful of them? Maybe? Same could be said for Poplar and Spruce Streets, too.

Trees used to be big business for New Bern, after all. Remember those lumber mills from before? I suppose in some ways lumber is still a business here: we've got the Weyerhaeuser and International Paper plants out on Washington Post Road. You do know why the road's called that, right? It's because they built the road on the old post road that used to run from here to Washington. That's Little Washington, mind you, not Washington, D.C.

Before I forget, I should say I've never understood the appeal for cats, myself. They're good for keeping down vermin, but they also kill the songbirds and even some snakes. There's a black snake around here, and if you ever see him, please don't kill him. He's the good kind, helping me take care of mice and rats and such. Anyway, maybe one day there'll come along a cat to change my mind, but I much prefer dogs. Dogs can point

and hunt and run deer, if you've a mind to train them, and provide
protection. I've known some good dogs in my day.

Back to Kelly and the tree. I suppose the two of us have more in common
than I'd care to admit.

When I was nine or ten - I'd have to have been that old because it was
after I'd fallen on the railroad tracks but before I suffered my bad bicycle
accident (another story for another time). Anyway, when I was nine or ten
I climbed a tree on Clark Avenue and then couldn't get myself down. I
forget why, since I can't remember being afraid of heights. Maybe this is
what cured me, or maybe there was something wrong with the branches
that I couldn't get a footing. Regardless, I'd climbed this tree and couldn't
get down. Someone ran and told my Mama, who called Daddy at work
down at the New Bern Municipal Water Plant, and he came along with a
few of his work fellows. Andy Shields climbed up into the tree with me
and had me hold onto his back while he climbed back down and set me on
the ground safe and sound.

If there's a moral here, I guess it's to never put yourself in a situation you can't easily get out of.

Take care for now.

Love,

Tom

Dear B.,

I was just watching a movie on AMC or TMC or something like that. At any rate, it was an old black-and-white film and some men had built a pit trap in the jungle. Maybe the movie was Tarzan? I don't know. I don't rightly remember much about the film except for them building this trap.

You know what a pit trap is? You need to dig a deep pit, deep enough that whatever you're after can't climb out once it's in. Some people put spikes in the pit. I wouldn't want to fall in one of those things myself. Well, after you dig the pit you cover it with vines or large leaves or something like that to camouflage what you've done so it looks just like the ground around it. I've never had to build a pit trap, but I did almost fall into one, or something like one.

When I was ten or eleven I was climbing a big tree that overspread a large ditch covered with bamboo vines.

Honestly, the bamboo down here is just awful. It's like the crazy mess from that Robin Williams movie: the writers had to have been thinking about southern cane. The stuff grows everywhere, clogs everything up and you've a bear of a time to get rid of it. In fact, I'd imagine even the bears around here would have some difficulty getting through some of the canebrakes I've seen out in the swamps. If someone could figure out how to get to the middle of one he'd have himself a nice hiding spot. If I remember right, that's exactly what some fellows did back in Prohibition.

There's even a story about two swamp men back in the late 1800s that supposedly shot a Bigfoot-like creature in a canebrake. They say the thing had been terrorizing people nearby, and these two fellows supposedly shot and killed the thing and brought it back to town. Then they shipped the thing off to be taxidermied - stuffed and mounted, you know - as they wanted to cash in on some reward or other being offered by the circus man P.T. Barnum. Well, story says these fellows shipped the hairy thing off and never saw hide or hair again. I say hogwash to the whole thing, but one never knows. There's strange enough stuff out there, to be sure.

As I was saying, I was climbing a big tree overhanging a large ditch covered with bamboo vines. From my last letter, you know trees and I don't exactly get along, and this time proved no different. I slipped and fell out of the tree, landing on top of the vines unharmed except for a few bruises. Now if I'd broken through that bamboo it might've been the end of me as this was a very large ditch and I fell about forty feet.

You might think I'm exaggerating, but I'm not. When I was up in that tree I could see over most everything, and I slipped and fell all the way to the bottom, landing on that pile of bamboo, which Daddy said probably saved my life, it being somewhat flexible and shock absorbent and such. I know one thing: I'm mighty glad I didn't end up in the ditch. It would've been my grave for sure.

I've got more stories about trees, but I'll save them for another time. I've probably worried you enough for one letter.

Love,

Tom

Dear B.,

There's an old saying that boys will be boys. But what will boys actually be? I suppose they'll be themselves. And when I was a boy, I did some very boyish things indeed.

* * *

I remember riding my bicycle one day - I might have been eleven or twelve at the time - along Metcalf Street and Louise Brady jumped in front of me and I hit her, throwing me over the handlebars and onto the stone walk. This was down by where the Tryon Palace is rebuilt today, right where the iron post is near the Jones House. Nearly parted my skull and required 16 stitches and I still have the scar today.

* * *

I often went hunting with Daddy, and early on he favored shooting a double barrel gun with hammers. We were crossing a fence and I pulled the gun through the fence. It caught and fired on one side close to my hand. Dad asked how it happened so I showed him and it fired the other barrel. I very nearly killed us both that day – no more hammered guns after that!

★ ★ ★

There's not much I wouldn't do for a bit of a treat, including stealing pecans over at the Crockett Farm. We were throwing sticks to knock down the pecans and I passed through an alley between their chicken house and garage. There was a fish box in the passageway, and I tipped it up so I could get a better throw. I looked down and saw a round iron plate. I touched it with my stick and it detonated, turning out to be a full size bear trap with teeth! It would have cut my feet off!! I guess old man Crockett was trying to catch a chicken thief, as he removed the box at night time.

★ ★ ★

On a dare I climbed the old Neuse River drawbridge to dive from the top into the channel. Tried to chicken out as it was really too high, but my buddies kept egging me on. So finally I just dived. My right leg hit a sunken log just at my knee, splitting it open. I was a long time healing as it got infected. We were at the hospital so much Dr. Patterson said I might as well get a room!

★ ★ ★

What boy doesn't like sports? We played lots of stickball and baseball growing up. Once on accident I hit my brother Bob with a baseball bat, hit him right in the head and thought I killed him. I didn't, but it was quite the scare nonetheless.

★ ★ ★

Now, you know I love going down to the water and feeding the pigeons, but do you know why? It's because the bell tower down at the Episcopal Church used to be full of them. Pete Hall and I used to climb that tower and catch pigeons and bring them home. Dad even built me coops and I raised pigeons for a bit. Another reason I don't chase them off from the feeders, either.

Speaking of Pete, his uncle lived right next door to the Catholic Church and School and somehow we began spying on the priest and the nuns. We'd watch them go down in the basement and the nuns would take of their habits and it turns out they were all of them as bald as could be! Then they'd drink, play cards, and smoke up a cloud.

They also had a chalkboard down there and we decided to climb down the coal chute to steal their chalk. While we were down there we heard them coming and I about got caught, but managed myself back up just in time.

* * *

Nuns weren't the only ones we'd make trouble for, either. We'd ride the trolley through town and rock it back and forth to throw it off the track. The Old Man - that's what we called the conductor, the Old Man - he'd never catch us but would run to his window and try to spit on us. Then he'd have to climb down and use a big iron bar to force it back on the track.

★ ★ ★

It's a wonder I survived growing up, what with all my shenanigans. But I did, and here I am telling you my stories.

Best stop for now before I run out.

Love,

Tom

Dear B.,

Vacationing wasn't a thing many people did around here back when I was a boy. You can be sure I jumped at the chance to take a cross-country trip with some friends of the family that were better off than we were. They had me along for company, the experience, and to help with the driving.

That's how, in 1934, I ended up at the World's Fair in Chicago.

Chicago. I don't remember much about the fair itself, but one night stands out more than most.

We were there the night John Dillinger was killed. We were just around the corner from a movie theater getting ice cream when we heard a pop and people started yelling and screaming. Ran to find out what was going on and saw Dillinger on the ground with several folks dipping their handkerchiefs in his blood. That's a sight I won't soon forget.

I really enjoyed the fair and the trip. Once out West we stayed in the Grand Hotel in Yellowstone Park. While going to dinner, I fell down the main lobby stairs, all the way from top to lobby floor. I had on white linen knickers and was really embarrassed, but only bruised a little. I was glad to move on to Washington, Oregon, California, and finally head for North Carolina.

I'd sent my girl Amber cards from all the states we visited. I wish somehow those cards survived, but so it goes.

Until next time.

Love,

Tom

Dear B.,

I joined the Navy in 1938. Left for boot camp on my birthday and nearly broke Mama's heart. Took a bus or train to Raleigh or Goldsboro and they had us new recruits bunk down. Put all these 17 and 18 year old guys together, most of them away from home for the first time, and they're bound to get in trouble. We got into a large pillow fight and destroyed all the pillows. They took those pillows out of our pay, too. First Navy paycheck and I didn't get hardly anything due to that night.

That wasn't the only time I got myself into trouble either. It's no secret I like bread; I've loved it as long as I can remember. Well, one day I was going through the mess line and managed myself an extra piece of white bread. I slipped it under my tray and made it all the way through the line when a sergeant called me out. "Poole! Show me that white bread!" I had to hold that piece of bread in the air the whole mess time while everyone else ate around me. Needless to say, I learned my lesson and never took more than one piece of bread after that.

I also got a Navy tattoo before my first leave and let me tell you, Mama was not pleased with that, either. I'm not sure which discouraged her more: me joining the Navy or that tattoo.

They say confession is good for the soul, and I feel good sharing these things, but I reckon that's about enough for today.

Love,

Tom

Dear B.,

In my last letter I told you how I'd joined the Navy. Well, this is the letter I think you've been waiting for quite some time now. I think I'm ready to talk about Pearl Harbor.

I've tried writing down my thoughts, but my mind gets so scattered thinking back on that day it ends up being unreadable. It's much better if I tell you about it, but you're not here to hear the story, and I've no one around to dictate to. So I wrote down what I could and looked back at a few newspaper write-ups and interviews I've given over the years. Being a Pearl Harbor survivor, I've become used to the attention every couple of years. Used to the attention; never used to the memory. Anyway, this next bit is a mix of my writing and two interviews I gave, one in 1955 and one in 1989. They're my words anyway, just written down by someone else - much like the rest of these letters, right? So, here we go.

After twelve weeks of boot camp I was assigned to the USS *Raleigh* (CL7). Ship and crew ordered to Pearl Harbor in 1939. I was still there in '41 when, on December 7, the Japanese launched their surprise attack against us in what history books call "Operation Hawaii" or "Operation Z". Of course, there weren't history books about the attack back then; it was current events, as current as could be.

That Sunday morning was probably no different on the *Raleigh* than on any of the other days. The sun is very bright at that time of the day there, and the air is so clear and fresh that the breezes seem to wash everything as they drift over the quiet water.

By the next morning, however, the skies were still full of smoke and the water was dirty with oil and wreckage from many ships. The *Raleigh* was on the bottom of the harbor with water lapping over the main decks and two gaping holes in her sides.

I was asleep when the alarm sounded about 6:55 for "General Quarters" and the word passed that the Japanese were attacking by air. With just enough time to pause to get my trousers on, I raced to my battle station in one of the four fire rooms.

The *Raleigh* was a four-piper cruiser with 12 boilers in all; a torpedo had hit near number 2 fire room and demolished six boilers at once. The fire room crews concentrated their efforts on keeping the remaining six boilers going to provide steam for the pumps (the ship was flooding) and generators supplying current to the guns.

I and my buddies soon found ourselves in a losing battle. The source of fresh water to supply the boilers was gone, and we had to use salt water from the harbor to make steam. Salt water leaves deposits inside the boilers as it turns to steam and soon closes the boiler tubes. It was a matter of using a boiler full blast until it clogged and burned up, then going on to another. With only six to start with, it didn't take long to run out of boilers.

I'd wanted to make the Navy my career. Of course, Pearl Harbor kind of decided that for me. I think Pearl Harbor was like a bad dream. There was a lot of concussion and a lot of confusion, people running here and people running there, bodies in the water and ships on fire. The *Utah* was tied next to us and had rolled over. I knew there were men trapped inside.

We cut a hole in the battleship's hull with acetylene torches and found another survivor. I remember he fell right on his knees and thanked the Lord.

Then the second wave of the attack came, strafers and dive bombers this time, and the ship was hit again. At this point I was helping man the guns, as engineers were assigned to assist handling ammunition. I and a guy named Williams were going to a gun station and he stepped through a doorway just as a 500-pound bomb came through the deck. Its fins hit him in the left shoulder and sliced it open. We dived for cover as the bomb passed through two more decks and exploded on the bay bottom below us. Lucky for us, as the tank we were hiding under contained a thousand gallons of aviation fuel!

The Japanese flew so close I saw one shake his fist at us and could see he was wearing a red tassel. I shook my fist back at him and wished I'd had a shotgun. Instead, we were sitting dead in the water. We kept firing, though, and were credited with downing six planes. We were the lucky ones, too. Williams, hit by a torpedo fin, and one other sailor who slipped on the deck and knocked his teeth out were our only recorded casualties on the *Raleigh.*

By this time the ship had taken a direct bomb hit to the stern or "fantail." Again the bomb failed to explode inside the ship but went on through and blew up underneath in the water. The *Raleigh* was already listing severely to starboard, and the underwater blast lifted her up and over to port. By this time also she was pretty far down in the water and was soon abandoned with decks awash.

After the attack, my shipmates and I stayed aboard for the next several weeks to begin the salvaging operation. It was a gruesome sight. They stacked all the bodies on an island which was also the fleet landing. Most were burnt beyond recognition.

Meanwhile, back in the States, my girl Amber heard by word of mouth that I'd died. We'd been childhood sweethearts, but drifted apart after I joined the Navy and was sent to Hawaii. Her family moved to Newport News, Virginia, where a friend told her I'd been killed. Now, I'd sent a Red

Cross telegram home telling folks I was alright, but it never came through. I made it home on survivors leave and found Amber on a blind date with a Marine in Ryman's drug store over in Bridgeton. "Tom Poole!" she said, "I thought you were dead!" I tell you she left that Marine sitting there alone. We were married the next week and she never left me again. I heard it once or twice that Amber was actually engaged to that Marine and she returned the ring to him that very night, but I don't know about all that.

Some people go back to Pearl Harbor every year. I don't want to go back to Pearl Harbor. In fact, I like New Bern. Despite all this, I wouldn't get my Pearl Harbor medal until 1957. When North Carolina began issuing Pearl Harbor Survivor license plates, I made sure to get one of those, too.

This is already the longest letter I've written and there's so much more to say. I think I'll stop here for now and write again after I've cleared my head a bit.

Love,

Tom

Dear B.,

Where did we leave off last letter? Amber and I married? I think that's right, but I feel I left something out, so let me back up a bit.

I told you I was assigned to salvage detail, but did I say we spent all that time sleeping on deck? We were making repairs to take her to a shipyard in California when I got orders for the USS *Massachusetts*, then docked in Quincy, MA.

That's when I got my 30 days survival leave, married Amber, and we moved to Boston. A whirlwind month, to be sure!

I spent the next weeks living in Quincy and going to the shipyard, where I became acquainted with new boilers and the engineers. Soon we were cleared to go to sea for a trial run to Bath, Maine.

The trial run over, Amber headed back to North Carolina and we were crossing the Atlantic to Morocco.

Have you seen the movie *Casablanca*? You know it was released during the war, right? In fact, it came out just after we liberated Casablanca. If you ever get the chance, watch it. Ingrid Bergman, I tell you what! I've only seen the movie a couple times. It brings back too many memories.

The fleet caught German battleships and the cruisers in their shipyard there in Casablanca. The *Massachusetts* sunk or damaged five ships in dry dock or in the shipyard, and we sunk two cruisers just out of port.

I remember our captain asking us to pray for the men we were about to attack. I haven't stopped. . .

After Casablanca we headed back to Norfolk for ammunition and fuel. And as we rested there in Norfolk, I'd also like to rest now.

Until next time.

Love,

Tom

Dear B.,

After resupply and R&R in Norfolk, we left the states and headed south and west. Passed through the Panama Canal and sailed on to the Pacific Islands via Pearl Harbor and Guam.

We operated there for the next year, during which time two notable things happened:

First, I officially entered the Realm of the Golden Dragon, and was inducted into the Silent Mysteries of the Far East. All of that's fancy talk to say I crossed the International Date Line for the first time. Used to be you'd get a colorful certificate with lots more wording, but this being the U.S. Navy in wartime, I got a small card with a little doodle. Still I kept it and later had it laminated.

There may have been more to the ceremony, but remember: the mysteries are silent, and on this, so am I.

The second thing that happened I've only told to a few people. Certainly no one in the Navy while I was still in the service.

You know I love the outdoors, and I took every opportunity to fish out there in the Pacific. One day we were out in a rubber dinghy and I decided to trawl a large shark hook I'd managed to get hold of behind us. Lord only knows what I'd have done if a shark actually took hold!

Anyway, I didn't get any fish, but wouldn't you know? That hook managed to put a decent sized hole in that rubber raft! They asked and threatened trying to find out who did it, but I let the hook over the side and never 'fessed up to what I'd done.

Eventually the Navy transferred me to destroyer duty, assigning me to the USS *Meredith* docked in Bath, Maine.

Of course, I didn't know it at the time, but had I stayed on the *Massachusetts* I would have been on duty during the battle of Leyte Gulf, now considered the largest naval battle in history. As it was, I missed it.

I sent a telegram to Amber on my way across:

OPK 1 & 2   14   San Francisco, Cal.   11:30 P.   Nov. 17, 1943

Mrs. P.J. Poole

350 Campostella Road

Campostella

Darling, flying across. Expect to arrive at airport Friday 19th at 9:30 A.M.   Love Tom

They misspelled my name, but it arrived just the same.

Amber found it too cold to go with me to Maine. As it was, I wasn't there for too long before we were headed out to sea on a shakedown run to Gitmo (that's Guantánamo Bay, Cuba) and then back up the coast to Norfolk.

Well, I've probably talked your ears off enough for one day, so I'll leave it off for another time.

Until then, take care.

Love,

Tom

Dear B.,

Last time we talked I'd just returned to Norfolk on the *Meredith*. Our ship was ordered to Plymouth, England in preparation of invasion of Europe. The *Meredith* was so new parts of her were still wet with paint - and we were sailing her into combat.

D-DAY / June 6, 1944

We were part of Operation Neptune, escorting ships and transports to Utah Beach and bombarding German positions overlooking the landing zone.

D-DAY +1 / June 7, 1944

We were hit by either a torpedo or a mine. At the time we thought it was a torpedo fired from a German U-Boat, but I think the official record says it was a mine. Either way, the *Meredith* was damaged, with over 50 sailors killed or wounded.

The plan was to tow us to safety to keep the *Meredith* from sinking, her being so new and all, but things don't always go according to plan.

D-DAY +3 / June 9, 1944 (11:30 AM)

Being slowly towed made us a prime target for attack. Down in the engine room, I thought we hit another mine, but they tell me a German plane dropped a bomb or torpedo on us and the ship broke or folded. To me it looked just like someone picked her up and folded her in half.

That night was the worst night in my life. Worse even than Pearl Harbor, worse than the day Amber died in 2006.

We floated in the water – in the dark and in the fuel.

I remember one sailor - I have no idea who he was – floating across from me and badly burned. He tried to give me a dog tag and rings to take to his wife. Some buddies floating near him thought I was robbing him and beat me off. By the time we cleared things up, the man had gone under and none of us saw him again.

Through the night, we could hear the cries and screams of others stuck in the cold waters of the English Channel as they cried out in hope and alarm as ships drew close. Some ships didn't hear the cries or see the men in the dark. I don't like to think how many were run over in the night.

All told, we lost over 100 personnel. A lot of things you'd like to forget. A lot of things you just put out of your mind.

Eventually I was picked up by the destroyer escort *Bates*. From there I was transferred to Scotland to await a ride home on the *Queen Elizabeth* as she headed to the States for repairs, being somewhat damaged herself. We arrived at New York Pier #92 a week later, and I headed home on accumulated 90 day leave, almost unheard of at that time. But it was true: I had two thirty day survivor's leaves and my annual 30 day pass.

I tell you, I rested well.

The afternoon is wearing on, and I'd like to rest again.

Take care.

Love,

Tom

Dear B.,

I don't have to tell you war is terrible, but I have no doubt this war was particularly awful.

I found myself assigned to USS *Oklahoma City* (CL-91) off the coast of Japan at war's end. Seven cruisers made the run into Tokyo Bay, firing at ships and bases. There was no return fire; we had beaten Japan to its knees.

The war over, I headed home on a long voyage via Saipan. September 1, 1946 - nearly one year to the day of V-J Day - was a Sunday. I kept the bulletin:

Saipan

aboard

USS TARAWA

Commanding Officer

Captain

Alvin I. Malstrom

U.S. Navy

Executive Officer

Commander

Robert W. Cooper

U.S. Navy

Chaplain

Commander

Fred D. Bennett

U.S.N.

Organist   George French Jr. S1c

LIFE

To the preacher life's a sermon;

To the joker life's a jest;

To the miser, life is money;

To the loafer, life is rest.

To the lawyer, life's a trial;

To the poet, life's a song;

To the doctor, life's a patient

That needs treatment right along.

To the soldier, life's a battle;

To the teacher, life's a school;

Life's a great thing to the thinker,

But a failure to the fool.

Life and long vacation to

The man who loves to work.

It is a constant effort to

Shun duty to the shirk.

To the faithful earnest worker,

Life's a story ever new;

Life is what we try to make it,

Brother, what is life to you?

Selected men desiring to sing in church choir, report after mess hall for opening get together at 1400.

Order of Worship

Prelude

The Call to Worship

Hymn No. 346

"I Love to tell the Story"

Fisher

The Invocation and the Lord's Prayer

Responsive Reading No. 38

The Gloria Patri

Hymn No. 534

"Shall We Gather at the River"

Lowry

Scripture Reading

St. Luke 22:1-30

Hymn No. 349

"Sweet Hour of Prayer"

Bradbury

Morning Prayers

Chaplain: *The Lord be with you,*

Congregation: And with thy spirit,

Chaplain: *Let us pray*

O Lord, show thy mercy upon us

Congregation: And grant us thy salvation,

Chaplain: *O God, make clean our hearts within us,*

Congregation: And take not thy holy spirit from us.

Prayer and Organ Amen

Baptism and Reception of Members

Communion Hymn. No. 236

"Break Thou the Bread of Life"

Sherwin

Holy Communion

Hymn No. 430

"Take the Name of Jesus with You"

Baxter

Benediction

Postlude:

On the back I scrawled this message:

Three new men confessed Christ this day and joined the church, so you see God is everywhere.

You should have heard me sing, as you can see I knew all of these songs except the last one.

★ ★ ★

Do you ever think it strange, the things we keep and the memories we cherish? These scraps of paper are worthless and priceless at the same time. It's all about perception. I guess we'll have to leave that question to the philosophers.

Love,

Tom

Dear B.,

Remember how I told you I joined the Navy on my birthday? Well, that meant I never actually graduated high school.

I served the Navy as an engineer and was entrusted with vital equipment and personnel and I wasn't even a high school graduate!

Thankfully, the Navy offered courses and I was able to complete my degree while in the service. Bridgeton High School even sent me an official paper certificate!

I never went to college; my experience in the Navy would prove to be enough to secure me worthwhile occupation once I returned to civilian life in the late 1950s. But that's a decade or so ahead of where we are in my story.

Having finally made my way stateside, I found I'd accumulated over 100 days of rehabilitation leave, and in the meantime was assigned to shore duty in Newport News, VA aboard the USS *Tidewater*. I put in for recruiting duty in North Carolina with these stations to recommend me:

USS *Raleigh*: fire room, engine room, and king

USS *Massachusetts*: fire room, evaporators, oil king

USS *Meredith*: in charge of fire room and auxiliaries

USS *Oklahoma City*: in charge of fire room and auxiliaries

USS *Tarawa*: in charge of fire room, evaporators, and oil king

USS *Bennington*: upkeep, maintenance, and preservation of machinery

Awards, Decorations, and Medals, including ribbons and operation and engagement stars:

Navy Good Conduct Medal and one bar

American Defense Medal with Ribbon and one star

American Area Medal and Ribbon

European, African, Middle Eastern Area Medal with Ribbon and one Star

Asiatic Pacific Area Medal with Ribbon and seven stars

Philippine Defense Medal and Ribbon

Victory Medal and Ribbon

The Navy granted me recruiting duty and assigned me to open a new station in Kinston, NC in the Sutton Building. Shortly after, I was put in charge of New Bern recruiting, where the papers made quite the fuss over their "local hero". I kept some clippings from the papers. These notices appeared in the New Bern Sun Journal:

Navy Recruiters Are On Permanent Duty Here Now

The Navy Recruiting Station which is being operated here on a five-and-a-half-days-a-week basis now has on its staff two chiefs with a total of 30 years of Navy recruiting behind them.

They are Chief Thomas J. Poole and Chief Leslie F. House. Chief Poole has been in the Navy for 18 years and his recruiting associate, Chief House, has been in the Navy for 12 years.

Chief Poole is a native of New Bern. He, his wife, and 13-year-old-son are making their home at 811 Williams Street here. Chief House is from Greenville and he and his wife and eight-year-old son are in temporary residence at 117 Peyton Avenue.

The two recruiters will be on duty in the basement of the local post office from 8:30 a.m. to 5 p.m. Monday through Friday and from 8:30 a.m. to noon on Saturdays from now on. They will be happy to answer questions and disseminate information about the advantages of a career in the Navy to any interested persons. They may be contacted at the Post Office or by calling Telephone 4971.

★ ★ ★

Native Son of New Bern Sent Here by Navy

Chief Boilerman Thomas J. Poole, U. S. Navy, has been assigned petty officer in charge of the Naval Recruiting station here, it was announced today by Chief Petty Officer Roy G. Ewell. Chief Ewell, who has been in charge of the station located in the post office building, is being transferred to Raleigh for further assignment to the fleet.

Chief Poole is a native of New Bern and said he is "mighty happy to be home." He enlisted in the Navy through the New Bern office in 1937 and is a veteran of both World War II and the Korean War.

Chief Poole has served in practically all types of naval vessels and states that he has seen his share of the world. A veteran of the attack on Pearl Harbor, he has received many medals and honors.

"I would be very happy to have all my old friends pay me a visit," Chief Poole said. "And, I'm also anxious to make new friends, particularly those interested in the United States Navy."

★ ★ ★

I was good at my job, and in 1956 received the following letter:

U.S.S. TIDEWATER (AD-31)

AD31/BSH:bb

P15

Ser: 513

6 June 1956

From: Commanding Officer, USS TIDEWATER (AD-31)

To: POOLE, Thomas J., BTC, USN

Subj: Recognition of outstanding recruiting services

Ref: (a) BuPers ltr ser Pers-B6-bjk ef 11 May 1956

1. It is noted with pleasure that your recruiting station won the distinctive title of "Station of the Month." We knew we had selected an outstanding TIDEWATER man when we nominated you for this job.

2. Reference (a) is quoted in part for your information:

"At the end of each month, one Navy Recruiting Station within each of the forty-three recruiting districts is designated as "Station of the Month." This award is based on the overall performance of duty of the personnel assigned. This is a distinct honor. The competition is keen. Many of these personnel are in charge of sub or branch recruiting stations. All of them are engaged in exceedingly important work. They are, in reality, choosing our personnel of the future."

3.   Keep up the good work. Congratulations and Well Done.

B. S. HANSON, Jr.

★ ★ ★

Well, I do believe that's enough back-patting for one day. Talk to you soon.

Love,

Tom

Dear B.,

It was about this time Amber and I moved to Madam Moore's Lane. This was long before that writer Nicholas Sparks put it in his books. We've had our share of goings-on around here, but nothing like what he writes about. Then again, as they say, truth is stranger than fiction. Some things you just can't make up.

We bought two back-to-back lots along the river, and started building thanks to my securing a home loan through the Equitable Life Assurance Society in '57 or so. My monthly payments were $90.52! That might seem cheap, but this was the late 50s. Jay tells me that's about $800 today.

We built the garage first and lived in that while we built the house. We moved into the house in '58, but the garage still got used. The Calvary Baptist Church met there when it first got started; now they're over on Rhem Avenue. Amber used it for years as a studio and classroom teaching art: ceramics and painting, mainly. Now it's used for storage.

I haven't been able to go through it properly in years - - who knows what's out there?!

Having retired from the Navy on December 15, 1957, on January 1, 1958, I took over my dad's job at the city water plant. I was also hunting and trapping, and building houses with F. Alligood.

In the 60s I went back to work on base at Cherry Point. This time I was a civilian working in the water treatment plant. I was the group representative, which meant that when we felt we were due a raise, it was up to me to make the argument. It wasn't just a matter of going to a supervisor and asking, we had to prove our point. I have enclosed my (successful!) request so you can see what we had to go through. I should warn you: it's fairly dull. It's OK if you only skim it. I promise I won't test you on it!

United States Marine Corps

Air Station

Cherry Point, North Carolina

November 18, 1966

TO: Director, Civilian Manpower Management, Department of the Navy, Washington, D.C. 20390

    Via: (1) Supervisor Water Treatment and Sewage Disposal Plants   Section

            (2) Director Utilities Division, Public Works Department, MCAS, Cherry Point, N.C.

            (3) Public Works Officer, MCAS, Cherry Point, N.C.

            (4) Commanding General, MCAS, Cherry Point, N.C.

            (5) Chief, Area Wage and Classification Office, Norfolk, Va.

            (6) Commander, Naval Air Systems Command, (AIR-4051)

FROM: Water Treatment Plant and Sewage Disposal Plant Operators, Utilities Division, Public Works Department, MCAS, Cherry Point, N.C.

SUBJECT: Pay Level Appeal for Water Plant Operators and Sewage Disposal Plant Operators Rating.

Ref: (a) ASO P 12000.6; Section F

(b) United States Code 10-USC-7474

1. With reference to that section of Ref. (b) as follows: "The Secretary of the Navy shall establish rates of wages for employees of each Naval Activity where rates are not established by other provisions of Law to conform as nearly as is consistent with the Public interest, with those of Private Establishments," the appeal for reconsideration of the present rating is considered justified.

2. There are no Establishments, either private or public, in the immediate vicinity by which rates may be compared with respect to the Quality and Quantity of Training and Knowledge required of the appealing encumbants.

3. The concerted efforts being made by Federal, State, and Local Health Authorities in the prevention of Water Pollution, the treatment of polluted water supplies and maintaining the high standards of potable water supplies,

also the treatment of Industrial Waste, requires that the encumbant personnel constantly participate in training programs within the Water Treatment and Waste Treatment field so as to be thoroughly capable to perform the duties, both technical and operational to conform to the Standards as required by the Health Agencies.

4. Training Programs in Water Treatment and Waste Treatment have and continue to be active, through the Activity Training Division, almost constantly since 1961, in efforts to keep abreast of Operational and Technical advancements and improved techniques, advanced knowledge in chemistry, hydraulics and mathematics. The knowledge derived from such training programs has become an absolute essential part of the qualifications of Water and Waste Works Personnel. Such qualifications are by this Activities Water Treatment and Waste Treatment Personnel through courses supplied by the Navy Department and programmed by the Station Training Division, in Basic, Intermediate, and Advanced Technology in the treatment of potable water supplies, Domestic Sewage and Industrial Waste.

5. It is mandatory that the encumbants of the position have a working knowledge of such bench trades as, plumber, machinist, electrician, etc. to make immediate repairs to treatment equipment in emergencies and on swing shifts when normal compliment of maintenance personnel are not available, to prevent interruptions in treatment processes as well as eliminate excessive loss in production and down time (i.e.; such as repairs as to Carbon Dioxide generating equipment, requires that the operating personnel dismantle pipes and tubing to 4" in diameter, replace and/or repair fuel burners and nozzles, replace electrodes, and repair or replace such items as relays on automatic warning devices, air compressors and gas dewatering equipment. Other items repaired include waste pumps, gas burners (Sewer), and chlorinators. Supervision of bench trades such as electrician, machinist, plumber, etc. when recalled to duty in extreme emergencies. The necessity to supervise such bench trades is that a thorough knowledge of the principles of operation and objective of the equipment to adequately repair and adjust to required specifications is needed, of which the average artisan has no knowledge.

6. In addition to the actual physical operation of the Treatment Plants, the operating personnel must perform analysis (chemical and physical) on both water and waste; and must interpret results of analysis furnished by laboratory personnel and make necessary changes and/or corrections to conform to proper and adequate treatment methods.

7. Not only do the Operating Personnel qualify in the normal duties and operating procedures, and unlike the bench trade artisan (i.e. welder, painter, truck-driver) who performs specific and repetitive duties requiring little knowledge of other trades or professions, the encumbants must plan, coordinate and make rapid changes in procedures, volumes and chemical contents of treated products, must anticipate the requirements of the consumer and adjust production accordingly. The encumbants must accept the responsibility of providing a product of their work which has a direct effect on the Health and Comfort of Activity Personnel. The margin for error in this profession is NIL.

8. During the normal 168 working hours each month, Operating personnel are without direct supervision for 120 hours. This is due to assignments to night shifts (rotating) week-ends and holidays. Although the Plant's Supervisor is available in emergencies (generally), the operating personnel normally make all decisions pertaining to operations (emergencies excepted) during these periods.

9. In view of the required scope of duties and responsibilities, it is deemed necessary to request reconsideration of the present pay level "9" for Water Plant Operators and Sewage Disposal Plant Operators ratings and request that the pay be aligned with positions of comparable responsibilities and duties, (i.e. Pay level "10 and/or 11").

Respectfully Submitted,

Thomas J. Poole, Operator
Water Treatment Plant Group
Representative

Appealing Personnel

The undersigned, through mutual agreement, have designated Thomas J. Poole, Water Plant Operator, as the appealing group representative.

William R. Poole

Horace L. West

Paul Howard

Julian A. Kaebuch

James L. Gardner

David W. Conway

Jackson H. Teage

Benjamin J. Smith, Jr.

Lauren L. Dayley

A. N. Holt

First Indorsement

1. Based on personal knowledge of the responsibilities and duties as well as the outstanding qualifications of encumbants, and from available information of comparable positions in Private Establishments which

indicate that generally a lesser degree of knowledge
and training is required, or, that personnel specialize
in single phases of treatment processes; whereas the
encumbants are skilled in all phases of their
occupation, am in concurrence with appellants request
in its entirety.

Charles A. Gould, Jr. Leading Operator
Water Treatment and Sewage Disposal Plants
Public Works Utilities Division
MCAS, Cherry Point, N.C.

★ ★ ★

With my military pension and two civilian incomes, I was finally able to
buy Amber the diamond ring she deserved. We settled on a wonderful half
carat set in gold from the Jewel Box on Middle Street. They aren't there
anymore, but I paid $139.95 taxes included, and I still have the Diamond
Guarantee Bond and the handwritten receipt to prove it.

Several years later, our family found itself in the papers again:

New Bernian Enlists in Airborne Group

Thomas J. Poole, III, son of Mr. and Mrs. Thomas J. Poole of Route 3, New Bern, left recently for Fort Jackson, S.C., to begin eight weeks of basic combat training.

According to Master Sergeant J. S. Yonick, local Army recruiter, Poole took advantage of the Army's "Choose It Yourself" program and chose to enlist in the 82nd Airborne division.

After completion of basic and advanced training he will then be assigned to the 82nd Airborne division for parachute training and subsequent assignments.

Poole's father is a retired Navy Chief and at one time was Navy Recruiter in New Bern. Mrs. Poole is known for her beautiful ceramic work and ceramic instructions.

$\star$ $\star$ $\star$

Well, you know the rest of that story and the sad situation he came to down in Alabama. I don't want to dwell on it here. Next time we'll talk of happier things.

Until then.

Love,

Tom

Dear B.,

I spent quite a bit of time outdoors in the last half century. I did it all: hunting, fishing, trapping - even eeling and turtling.

I was good at it, too. I wrote a pamphlet on trapping that was for years published by a hunting magazine. I think it was *Outdoor Life*, but I can't be sure. I don't have any copies left myself, and Jay couldn't find anything online. Maybe someday one will turn up.

The Japanese bought my eels; a bit of irony in that, I think. I pulled them in right off my dock down by the water, the dealer bought them from me, and I'm told they were on the market in Japan within 36 hours. Not bad for a New Bernian, eh?

I do have one funny story about turtles, and unlike that Jack Sparrow fellow in *Pirates of the Caribbean*, this one's true. My partner and I were taking a load of turtles up somewhere in Virginia and stopped for lunch. When we came out, somehow our cage had come open and our turtles were escaping! I'm not sure if we left it unlatched by accident or if someone came by and opened it. We got most of them back, but lost more than a few.

The river is a harsh mistress, and I've had my own share of close calls. One time I took the boat out to Island Creek in search of otters. I found a bank otters were using as a slide, so that's where I decided to put out a drowning wire. Since the bank was steep, I had to lie down and set the trap in the slide run itself. I wedged my foot in a root for support while I set the trap underwater. This was really cold work, but I had on rubber gloves.

All of a sudden, the root broke and I slid over the trap, which caught me by my clothes and belly! This was a big trap, and I couldn't compress the springs. I finally managed to get my pliers on the bank, cut the wire, and with the trap still gripping my stomach, headed home. It was about a 6 mile ride, and hurting at that!

I found my trap setter in the boat house, and my brother Bill helped get that trap off my belly. Lots of bruises but no infection – really it could have been much worse. Poured an entire bottle of peroxide on my belly and that was that.

Not everyone was so lucky, but I also helped pull more than a few folks out of the water over the years. Too many people go out without a life preserver or knowing how to swim.

Anyway, I've just remembered a few more outdoor stories for you. I'm getting to like this talking business.

★ ★ ★

One day we went rabbit hunting in what is now the Trent Woods area, just across the creek bridge. There were four of us as we stopped to pick up a black fellow in Pembroke since he had a couple of dogs. We were all crossing a field in a line about 10 yards apart and a rabbit jumped up between me and the man we'd picked up. He swung his gun in my direction and fired, knocking my cap off. One pellet hit me in the head, five others in the cap. Three inches lower and it would have blinded or killed me. Really a close call. I went to the doctor and he said to leave the pellet in for a while. Thirty years later Dr. Bobbitt removed the pellet, which turned out to be #4 shot. The place won't heal completely. It looks like I've a mole on my head, but it's just skin from that pellet.

* * *

When we were kids, maybe ten to fifteen years old, we used to put on rabbit drives. My favorite gun to use was the .410 shotgun or .22 single shot rifle. We lined up across a field and walked slow, kicking every thicket. If a rabbit was found, you would holler "There he goes!" The purpose of the line was to keep game out in front, with strict instructions to stay in line.

On this hunt were Chester Besh, Eddie Paul, and Robert and David Brinson, and myself. A rabbit was jumped, I had a shot, and as I pulled the trigger, Eddie, who had left the line and crossed a ditch, hollered "I'm shot!"

We all ran to him and saw the bullet had glanced ground and hit him crossways on the chest, leaving a blue streak about a quarter inch wide across his chest between his nipples.

We took turns carrying him to the road where we hailed down Mr. Ray Doughtery, who took him to the hospital where the bullet was removed. He and we were fortunate the bullet went across and not straight in. Though Eddie has passed on now, for years we both lived as neighbors on Madam Moore's Lane.

This hunt took place about where the Wal-Mart and strip mall is now.

★ ★ ★

I've got a few more stories in me, but that's about all I can manage for now.

Until next time, then.

Love,

Tom

4-6-82

Dear Ricky Dupree,

Enclosed is information you requested, but I suggest you keep it to yourself. You'll be surprised. This method of catching these "snappers" really works and there is a market available. At present, I am selling to Hazelwood Bros., Lanexa, Virginia 23089. The price last year was $.45 per pound, live weight. They will take them from 4 pounds and up. These snappers must be handled carefully as they are afraid of nothing and are capable of removing a finger.

The rig I use is Pole and Line equipped with a #6 O'Shannesy hook. This hook has a large area, making it easy to tie, also right size to keep sliders and smaller turtles off. Of course, if you want to catch smaller ones and there is a market for them, go to a smaller hook. The pole is a reed about six to eight feet long, 1/2 to 3/4 inches diameter or even smaller. The end is sharpened as enclosed sample. The line is tarred nylon as per sample, or braided nylon. Buy this in spools, it's cheaper. Be sure and clean reed at joints as growths can hurt your hand.

Line has to be at adjusted to depth at setting, to keep bait on bottom, yet allowing turtles to swim to top after being hooked. Now for the secret, the Bait!! It is salt eel, cut into pieces about 2 inches long. I salt overnight and bundle my poles, twenty-five to the bundle, tied with bands cut from inner tubes before leaving house. This way, I know how many poles I have set and by untying only one bundle at a time I can set them as boat runs along shore without tangles. I put out poles about 5 to 10 feet offshore 20 to 30 yards apart. If pole is missing check ashore as most of the time larger turtles will pull the pole and all to shore. Several times I have caught over 5 to 600 pounds a night.

Set your poles along marshes, mouths of slews; creeks are best places for larger turtles. Some will go 30 to 40 pounds. You adjust slipknot to water as you stick pole into bottom. Length of line is about 5 feet. Notice knot used in sample. Always, always hook eel on hook through back and push hook clear through to expose barb. "Brother Snapper" will swallow whole piece, and barb must be exposed to hook him in throat.

The boat I use is a 14 foot Pram type of boat with shallow draft. This works fine for me as the tide here at times is a problem.

You will need large mouth burlap bags, a long handled sharp knife and a rack, (if turtling alone) to hold bags. After catch, lead the turtle to boat gently by string, grab him by the tail, turn him over on back and cut string at mouth, leaving hook in mouth. Some hooks can be recovered, not many. Hooks can be replaced then or later.

The rack I use is a cross type board with hooks on cross-arms and clamps to boat seat. This holds bag at two sides and when I lift turtle to put in bag, I pull out bag with left hand and drop turtle in bag. I usually put three to a bag or four smaller ones. Tie bag with long strips of rubber inner tube. Turtles will settle down shortly.

I keep turtles in a pen filled with old sawdust about 2 feet deep. Keep material damp. They will dig out, so you must have wire, cement bottom, etc. to keep them in. Make sure your pen is strong as they will climb and dig. Do not put them where they can swim as they lose too much weight.

There will be times you will find one hung up on a stump or root. He may look dead but many can be "pumped" back to life if he hasn't been drowned too long. Lay him on his back and press plate up and down. You may save that twenty dollars!! If he revives, put him off to himself until he is strong again.

I run about 200 calls a day. Set poles before sunset and get back to them early. Nothing beats looking up the side of a bank and seeing four or five poles shaking. Approach poles slowly as sometimes there will be a large male atop a smaller female and you can catch him by the tail first. Had this to happen several times.

Time was I could supply poles ready-made for $.50 each (FOB) but sorry, freight is just too high. I have gone out of the pole business for now.

GOOD LUCK TURTLING!!!! Write if you need any more information and send stamped SAE.

Trapper Tom

Dear B.,

Trying to capture a lifetime of family in a few short pages is nearly impossible. People, lives, and memories are funny things as they are so intertwined.

Long after we became adults and married, Amber and I continued to enjoy time with our brothers and sisters and their families; sometimes we even vacationed together.

I remember especially the visits from Amber's sister Jean, along with her husband Marvin, and their children, Amber Sue and Marvin Anson. Yes, there'd be times two Ambers were in the house! I affectionately called my niece Amber my "blond headed terror", which she loved.

Now, some of the names in our family might get confusing. I married Amber Catherine Liverman, sister to Jean (sometimes called Betty Jean) and Bruce (known as Buddy). Bruce married Frances Gray and they had three children: Debbie, Teresa, and George. Jean married Marvin Malish and they had two children: Amber Susan and Marvin Anson. Jean's Marvin was the only one of our group that didn't grow up together with us: he was from Texas and met Jean while in Newport News, Virginia. We called Amber Susan "Amber Sue" and Marvin Anson "Buddy". If that weren't confusing enough, there was another relative in the mix we also called Buddy. Somehow we managed to keep them all straight.

When school let out they headed to one of two places: the lake house or our house here on the Trent River. Jean told us that when they'd cross the border into North Carolina, she'd tell the kids to take their shoes off - they were in the Tar Heel State!

It was always a great adventure having them visit. While the sisters laughed and talked in the house, I'd take the kids down to the river to crab, fish, or swim. Sometimes they'd step on sand spurs on the way to the water, and I'd scoop them up and carry them the rest of the way. The distance from the house to the water can feel like miles if your feet are hurting.

Both Amber Sue and Marvin could swim, but I wouldn't let them in the water without an adult. The river currents can be sudden and tricky. There was a tree that grew right up out of the water next to the pier. After all these years it's actually grown around the handrail! Back then I had a boat house right next to the tree, and there were rails so I could winch my boat up and down. There was also a small, sandy beach that sloped out into the water, making it easier for swimming. Over the years the river's changed and the sand washed away, so that now there's only the rocky beachhead left. You can still see some sand if the tide is out far enough.

The kids were curious about the bomb shelter Bill and I built after the war. We built it at the same time we dug out the room under the den in the main house, so sometime in the 60s. I've got a pamphlet around here somewhere that we used when we built it. We let the kids peek inside, but never let them go in and play.

Bill and Helen were our neighbors on one side, the Bennetts on the other. Mack Franklin Bennett owned a series of laundries in the area, notably the City Laundry in downtown New Bern, and their house had a trench in the yard left over from the Civil War. They let Amber Sue and Marvin play in the moat, sliding down the sides and looking for relics after storms. More than once they told me our home by the river was the coolest place on earth.

Amber Sue's father had taught her and her brother how to fish, but here in New Bern we've brackish water, which can be a fun and different experience for someone who's only fished freshwater. Sometimes, they'd catch an eel. They'd yell and I'd run over and get it off their hooks. If I was lucky, I'd be able to save it to sell. Other times there'd be a fish they couldn't get off the hook, and I'd get to help them yet again.

Sometimes we'd go crabbing. I'd have Amber save chicken necks in the freezer and thaw them out just before a visit. I'd put hooks through the necks and the kids and I would go out on the water and toss the bait over the side. The kids would hold onto the strings and I'd help them pull up and net the crabs. If they were large enough, and if we caught enough, Amber would cook them up for dinner.

Well, all this talk of fishing and crabbing has made me hungry. I guess I'll close for now.

Until next time.

Love,

Tom

Dear B.,

I taught the kids to clam, scallop, and shuck. I also taught them how to shoot with small bows and arrows, how to spot squirrels' nests, and how to identify animal tracks and various plants like mistletoe.

They weren't the only ones to enjoy the outdoors with me. Sometimes Amber's sister Jean would go out frog gigging with me. She'd gone gigging as a little girl and knew just how to hold the light. I didn't let the kids go out - they were too little at that time. That didn't stop them from waiting up for us and listening to their mom tell all about how we'd bagged our mess of frogs.

Speaking of Jean, at that time I had a relatively large garden on the road side of the house. That's the side everyone drives up on, but it's technically the back of the house. Waterfront property means the front of the house faces the water. Most everyone gets that wrong. After these many years I'm used to it.

Back to the garden. Jean and the kids would help me pick the fresh produce, mainly tomatoes and cucumbers in those summer months. One summer, we were picking in the garden and Jean lost her engagement ring. We looked and we searched and I even borrowed a metal detector from a friend, but we never did find that ring.

I'm certain our home was at times nothing more than organized chaos. There'd be pelts from animals I'd trapped, eels I caught and sold for pickling, light wood I'd gather from the forest and use for my own fires or sell to campers, duck decoys, and even turtles which I sold to the Campbell's soup people in the 60s and 70s.

I recall a particularly smelly trip to deliver turtles, and I stopped by to see Jean and Amber Sue and the two Marvins. I stayed the night and washed out my truck. Laughing, I swore I'd never do that again, but of course I kept turtling into the early 80s until the demand for turtles died off due to protection laws. It was just as well, as by that time my arthritis was making turtling difficult.

But, I did what I had to do in order to provide.

I know you know me as a hunter, but for years I only hunted with a bow. It just wasn't fair to the deer if I used a gun. I set up a target halfway between the house and the water to keep in practice.

With the help of family we built our share of decks, room additions, tears, and even the original bulkheads for the lake house. It wouldn't have been a surprise to see us outside working in shorts, heavy socks and boots, and no shirts.

Once or twice we bought a wooded lot, hunted or trapped what we could, cleared the land of timber, and then re-sold the lot. Once we even build a spec house and were quite pleased when it sold.

We brothers and brothers-in-law were quite different, but we shared many of the same values. I reckon that's why we got along with each other so well.

I have a few more such stories to tell, but I've written enough for today.

Talk to you soon.

Love,

Tom

Dear B.,

I'm still thinking about those family visits.

One time I'd had a successful deer hunt and still had it hanging in the boat house when Amber Sue came by. She was at that young, curious age, and rather than shooing her off I asked if she'd be upset to see the deer.

She told me it wouldn't, so I let her watch me clean and skin the carcass. I carefully explained each step so she would understand what I was doing, and how that deer would be our dinner some night.

I have a great love for children and animals, balanced with a terrific gift for living off the land. I remember Amber making a deal with me back when we were first married: whatever I caught and cleaned, she'd figure out a way to cook it. She was incredibly successful! Our freezer was always stocked with fish, venison, you name it - she cooked it all, including frog legs.

I never liked killing for the sake of killing. But I did love being in the woods hunting deer or out on the water fishing or running a trap line. There was always something to keep me busy.

But oh, how I loved to tease Amber, too! On one of the most memorable times, we were in the kitchen and she passed by me. Instinctively, I reached out, patted her bottom, and commented that there was a little more of her to love. She blushed but quickly came back and said there was a little more of me to love as well.

Of course I couldn't let that go, so I stood up, sucked in my stomach, pushed out my chest, and loudly proclaimed I looked exactly the same I always had. She laughed and got the last word when she said she'd see how long I could hold my breath. Of course that was enough to make everyone laugh and I quickly lost that challenge!

We had many happy mornings around that kitchen table. I have something of a sweet tooth, but never for chocolate or chocolate cake. Chocolate takes me back to my Navy ration days, when our kit included chocolate and cigarettes. I gave up that awful habit years ago, but the taste of chocolate brings it all back.

Anyway, to satisfy my fondness for sweets, I'd often start my mornings with a big bowl of frosted flakes. Now it might have been the sugar talking, but when the kids were over I just had to make them laugh. Remember that tattoo I'd gotten in the Navy? Well, I'd placed both hands on my head and flex my biceps, first left then right, and I'd make that anchor go up and down! The kids would nearly fall out their chairs howling with laughter, while Amber would be slightly embarrassed. She'd blush a bit and call me out - Tom POOLE! - but then she'd look at the kids and start laughing, too.

I suppose someone looking at our marriage would never call it commonplace. Amber's eyes would twinkle, and I would do my absolute best to get her blushing, and when we had visitors over I'd wink at them while Amber wasn't looking just to get a laugh.

Laughter really is the best medicine! Laughter and love. Amber and I tried to spread our love to everyone who came under our roof.

I hope everyone could have just as good a love story as Amber and I had been blessed to have.

Sometime I might tell you a little about some of the trips we took.

Until then, take care.

Love,

Tom

Dear B.,

I promised to tell you more about our family trips. Sometimes we'd go up and see Amber's family in Virginia for Thanksgiving or Christmas. Bruce and Frances lived in Newport News and Marvin, Jean, and Nettie Susan lived in Hampton. We'd all gather at Jean's house, usually arriving just in time for Marvin's Christmas office party.

They all knew I didn't like leaving the woods or river for very long, so when I went to visit, Marvin and I would go to Sears to look at tools. Later on we'd also look in at Lowes and the Bass Pro Shop.

Sometimes Amber would visit her folk without me. She'd always cook enough ahead of time for my meals, though I'd also take a few trips down to Hardee's for breakfast and a hamburger. She even made desserts for me! One thing she avoided was garlic. I hate the smell of it because it reminds me of the war and our Italian allies throwing up on deck. If Amber used garlic at all she'd sneak in just a little bit or avoid it altogether.

They'd also take trips when Amber's family visited us. After getting all caught up at the house, I'd head off to the hunting club while Amber and the rest went to visit other relatives or go shopping in Beaufort or Emerald Isle. They even went as far as Wilmington on occasion! Amber would pack them a lunch, usually pimento cheese sandwiches packed in a bread wrapper and thrown in a cooler on those hot summer days. I tried to be good about giving her time with family, but at the same time she never neglected taking care of the house.

On Sundays we all went to church together, unless someone was travelling home.

There were times when all our families met up at the lake house, and as some of Amber's family had places there, there was plenty of room for everyone.

We'd spend some time working on improving the properties. We might add on rooms or build piers or run water lines. We were fortunate in that between all of us we could do almost anything that needed to be done, and if we couldn't do it, we'd learn how.

We played just as hard as we worked; enjoying fishing, swimming, or just putting puzzles together on the table. We had to stop playing the game "Aggravation" when Amber didn't like being sent back spaces, which of course was the point of the game and my delight to do.

With all these stories you might wonder about Amber and me. All my picking on her was good-natured and always ended with the two of us laughing: never a doubt it was all in fun. Amber kept nearly everything I sent her while in the Navy, like little handmade flowers from Italy or a mechanical "yes/no" monkey she kept in its box high on a shelf and only pulled down on special occasions.

I recall one hot, humid night at the lake house we adults decided to go skinny dipping. It was pitch black with no lights, not even from the stars, and we set some rules: menfolk first, women after. The girls stayed up at the house, and when we men came back inside after cooling off, all the girls went down, even the younger ones – who I'm told enjoyed splashing around and scaring off the fish. Of course we couldn't keep ourselves from joking them, and so we'd call out as if we were coming back down to join them, causing everyone to squeal and howl with laughter.

During the day I'd take the kids swimming, and they loved seeing how long I could hold my breath. I'd dive off the pier and they'd start searching for me. About the time they'd start worrying, thinking no one could stay under that long, I'd pop to the surface, laughing. I'd be so far from where I went in they just didn't believe it was possible. I tried to keep my sense of humor and to always have a funny story to tell the kids. Some nights we'd watch the news or a television program together.

Amber and her sister Jean loved to paint. I think I've told you this before, but they both painted canvasses and Amber painted ceramics while Jean preferred china. Sometimes they'd even paint rocks or seashells, and as they painted they'd nearly fall over with laughter at the silly creatures they came up with. They often did more realistic work, too. I remember one time I saw a picture of a deer I quite liked, and wouldn't you know Jean painted that deer for me for Christmas? Another time she painted me a rather risqué mermaid – a nod to my time in the Navy. Amber Sue tells me her mother giggled the whole time she painted it, that mermaid sitting with her arms crossed in just the right places for modesty. If I recall rightly, she painted one for her brother Bruce, too.

I wonder what you'll think of me after all these stories, or what you might remember. I hope you'll remember Amber and I loved God and our family, and had hearts to help those in need. It was our faith that kept our marriage together, for without God I'm not certain we would have made it many years.

We had our share of struggles. We wanted children, but after several miscarriages Amber had a hysterectomy. So, we doted on everyone else's children. Our love for each other was strong – our love for God, stronger.

There were many friends, neighbors, church folk, and hunting club buddies whose friendship I treasured. I always tried to speak kindly of them and never speak ill of anyone, even those I had difficulties with. I tried never to use foul language or treat Amber or the womenfolk or the children in any way that wasn't honorable. That's not to say we weren't mischievous or hilarious – we were! – but at the same time, none of us were perfect. We tried to bring the good into the family. I once heard it said all the men in our family set the bar so very high it was hard for other men to measure up.

High praise, indeed. I never went out of my way to be anyone's role model.

Heaven knows I have problems of my own. But I suppose it's inevitable that we shape folks around us, whether we like it or not. I suppose you might say Amber and I were quiet influences, praying our love for God and for one another would be evident to those around us. If we were a blessing to someone or made a difference or encouraged them to live a godly life, then that's enough for me. What more could I ask for than to leave someone better off for having known them? I didn't ask for any of this praise. If Amber and I made such a difference, it's all because of God.

Until next time, then.

Love,

Tom

Dear B.,

I was thinking about a couple who used to go to our church; they lived down below Harkers Island. Do you remember them? No?

Well, one day I was down on the Island hunting or some such and I came down a path to the water. Fellow came up in a boat and called out to me:

Did you come down that path?

Yeah

I wouldn't walk down that path for a thousand dollars.

Why not?

Place is full of ticks. You might wanna go and check yourself there.

I pulled up my pants leg and you couldn't even see skin it was so black with seed ticks. I had over a hundred of them on my back - so many I felt I was all stitched up, couldn't even move my arms without it pinching and pulling there were so many of them.

I went to the doctor for a shot and to get checked over and she said

Tom, this is what you do. Go and get you some green alcohol and dissolve 24 aspirin in it. Then get Amber to spread that wherever you've got a tick.

So I did just that and I tell you what, when Amber used her cotton swabs to spread the stuff out it was like those buggers all just released and it killed them outright. I could breathe again.

So now if you ever get in some ticks you know just what to do. Take care.

Love,

Tom

Dear B.,

The older I get, the faster time goes. I've blinked and 30 years have passed. I retired from the city and the base. I spent more time out of doors and more time with Amber. I'm glad I did.

Amber started going downhill in the late 1990s or early 2000s. We hadn't been apart since I came home from the war, and I wasn't about to start now. So I looked for a caregiver - someone to come in and look after her for a few hours and do some light housework.

That's how I got to know you and your family. Pastor Wingard gave me your name and you graciously came in and treated Amber with the care and dignity she deserved. You were there for several years until her home going on December 6, 2006, just one day off from Pearl Harbor. That time of year will always be difficult for me.

Thank you for staying with me. Though Amber was gone, you still came in and kept house for me. You made sure I had someone to talk to. Jay and

Krystal would come over to visit during college breaks, and Jay even interviewed me for his senior paper. I think I already told you that.

You and your family often came over for supper and to play Aggravation. I don't know which was more aggravating: the game itself or the fact that I had a bear of a time convincing Jerry and Jay to kick you or Krystal back to start. More often than not, it was "girls rule and boys drool".

When hurricane Irene came through in 2011, I got the chance to return your kindness just a little when you came to stay with me. You were checking on me, but I was able to have your back as your neighborhood flooded and went without power for some time.

Truth be told I got used to having you around. When I asked if you'd move in to help me full-time, you did.

You will never know how much that meant to me. To be able to grow old in the house I've built with my own hands, where Amber and I lived for so long, where I have so many pleasant memories - - words cannot describe my gratitude.

You've stayed with me ever since. We've celebrated birthdays and holidays, played games and watched movies, and eaten many a good meal together.

True, I've had my fair share of problems. My hearing is shot and sometimes I don't take my medicine properly. How many times you've struggled to get me into bed after I've fallen asleep at the table! But apparently I've given you a few laughs as well. I recall you telling me I'd ask you to dance even though I was not capable of doing so.

My heart is full from the blessing you've been. How many good years you must've added to my life - you and the pets Sarah's brought into the house. Pushing Kona the cat around on my walker or trying to keep Indy the dog from stealing my tissues has added a new level of joy and excitement in my old age. Sarah's also been a good one to talk sports with. She likes boxing and wrestling and a lot of the sports that other people don't particularly care for.

Thinking back on all this, you can bet your bottom dollar I'll go to sleep with a smile on my face.

Hopefully not at the kitchen table.

Until we talk again.

Love,

Tom

Dear B.,

This is the letter you've been dreading: the last letter I will ever write. You and I both knew this day was coming, but knowing something doesn't always make the experience any easier.

I'm old, Barbara. I'm old and I've lived a long, full life - and it's been both longer and fuller because you and your family were in it. What other ninety-eight year old man can say they passed away in the house built by their own two hands and surrounded by folks he knows love him? Too many die in nursing homes with family long gone or long forgotten. Others have family - or what passes for it - that can't wait for the old codger to die so they can get their hands on what's left them.

I haven't had to worry about any of that. You have cared for me beyond expectation, and I'm thankful for you.

Sure, there are things I'd still like to see. I'd like to see Sarah married. I'd like to see Jay and Krystal have a child - all in God's time of course, and I'd never say such a thing out loud. I'd like to watch Duke win another basketball championship.

But I'm like a child again, waiting up on New Year's Eve. The excitement of the ball dropping in Times Square and the desire to see the New Year rung in just can't compete with the tiredness inside, and he falls asleep long before midnight.

I'm tired, Barbara.

I'm tired of the fighting. I helped Mama and Daddy fight the Depression. I fought the Japanese and the Germans in World War II. I fought to make a better life for Amber and our family. I fought this land to build a house. I fought the woods and the river to provide. I fought time and, for decades, I've won. I've fought chronic pain in my back and shoulder, I've fought declining eyesight, and I've fought off disease and kept this aneurysm at bay for years. But no man can fight forever.

I once said that if I lived to be a hundred I'd run around the yard naked. Looks like that won't be happening, and perhaps for that we should all be thankful.

I've fought as long as I can. I've fought as long as I wanted to. But now, I want to rest. I don't want you to think I'm giving up. I don't want you to think I'm abandoning you. I'm just choosing to stop fighting. I'm leaving on my own terms. I know you don't like this DNR hanging above my bed. I know you don't like this bed, period - this hospital bed is a far cry from the wood and metal frame I've slept in for years. But this is what I have chosen, and now you won't have to worry anymore.

I've known for some time now this would come sooner rather than later. I've made provisions so you won't have to do a thing. Everything's spelled out in black and white, bought and paid for years ago. A phone call will put it all in motion. I know there's paperwork I can't do that will be left for you to do, but I've made things easy as I can.

I want to go. Already I'm slipping away. My mind, once kept sharp by those lists, is fractured. I can't remember names. The other day I called Jerry "that catfish man" or some such thing. I don't want to forget everything in the end. I want to hold on to something.

I've said my goodbyes. I started them when I took this turn last November. I know people still come and visit and some talk to me even though I can't say anything back. Jay comes and sits with me and holds my hand. I don't know what he's saying. I think he's praying in German to focus his mind on something other than this. And that's OK. We talked before all this happened. He's going to write my story for me. That book you always said I should write? It's his now. I think he doesn't say anything to me because the last time we talked I thanked him for being my friend, that I counted it a privilege to have known him. I think he wants to remember me as I was and not as I am. I think we all want that.

I know where I'm headed, Barbara. I can see their shining faces in the doorway while you care for me, and they watch over me in the night, singing such sweet songs as you cannot imagine.

My eyes grow heavy. You've said I can leave when I'm ready.

I'm ready now, but I don't want you to see it.

Could you leave the room for a minute? Would that be all right?

I'm so very tired. Take care.

I Love You,

Tom

Thomas Judson Poole Jr.

NEW BERN | Thomas Judson Poole, Jr. passed away peacefully at his home, surrounded by loved ones, Friday, February 03, 2017.

Thomas was preceded in death by his loving wife Amber Poole.

He served his country faithfully for over 20 years in the United States Navy.

Thomas was fortunate to survive both Pearl Harbor and D-Day.

He continued his service to country as a civil servant at MCAS Cherry Point for another 20 years.

His family and loved ones will receive friends at Pollock-Best Funeral Home, Tuesday, February 7, 2017 from 1:00pm to 2:00pm. A funeral service for Thomas will immediately follow at 2:00pm in the Pollock-Best Funeral Home Chapel. Burial in Greenleaf Memorial Park will follow.

In lieu of flowers donations may be made in Thomas Poole's honor to Calvary Baptist Church, 1821 Rhem Ave, New Bern, North Carolina 28560.

Arrangements entrusted to Pollock-Best Funerals and Cremations.

Requiem

Dear Reader,

I was teaching when I got the call Mr. Tom was passing. In fact, he passed while the call was being made. I'd been prepared for this: I'd made out lesson plans two weeks ahead of schedule and told the school office that I would need bereavement leave on short notice. All I had to do was pick up my stack of papers, tell the office I was gone, and walk out the door.

I arrived at Mr. Tom's house and went in to see him. He was at peace, like he'd just fallen asleep and might wake up at any time. And yet, I knew he was gone and would not be returning. So I knelt by his side and said all the things I'd said to him before he passed, hoping that somehow God would allow his spirit to linger a little and clearly hear the words his loved ones wanted him to hear.

I thanked him for being my friend. I thanked him for finding me work when I first moved to New Bern. I thanked him for all the times I'd needed help and he stepped in. I thanked him for talking to me about all the things he'd seen and done. I thanked him for treating me like a son, and, before I rose, recalled these words from Dante:

Before you now appears the militia of Christ's triumph.

I would say we laid Mr. Tom to rest, but the truth is he was at rest already. We carried out his final wishes exactly as he wanted:

Order of Service

Opening Prayer and Words by Pastor Dwight Williams

Bible Reading of Psalm 23, Mr. Tom's favorite passage of scripture

"The Old Rugged Cross", sung by Glenda Daniels

Reading of "The Man with Many Hats" by Jay Eldred

Mr. Tom - The Man with Many Hats

by Barbara Bloomberg Rowe

The first hat was special to Mr. Tom because it was given to him by Sarah

who chose this hat because of the deer embroidered on the side. This hat

captured the embodiment of a man who truly loved the outdoors. He was

a true sportsman who was always full of adventure. Mr. Tom was a daring

huntsman and fisherman- the list could go on and on. He was devoted to

the outdoor sports and recreational activities such as hunting, fishing,

trapping, turtling, eeling, and much more. He was a true outdoorsman as

well as a great provider and hard worker. He turned his outdoor sports

into a way to provide food and money for his family.

The next hat Mr. Tom had was this crazy hair hat. This hat captured

another side of this wonderful man's humorous personality. You didn't

have to be around him long before this personality trait would show forth.

Even in these last few weeks through the pain, he would still joke and smile at family, friends, nurses, and anyone who took a few minutes to stop in and say hello.

The third hat is the Duke basketball cap. Yes, this man enjoyed watching any type of sports. Basketball was his favorite, but Duke was his team. He wore his hat when his team played, and win or lose, he was a devoted fan. This hat was Mr. Tom's dress hat. When he wore this hat, he was very distinguished. He wore it well, and he wore it with honor, dignity, and respect. These personality traits were what we saw when he wore this hat. He was full of integrity, trust, patriotism, and Godliness. He loved his family, and we loved him.

The last hat represented is his Navy hat. Chief Thomas Poole was a person who served his country well and also respected the US Navy with pride and honor. We recognize his life today as a devoted patriot, a brave and proud sailor, who was both honest and true. He served on 6 ships while in the Navy. His first post of duty was on the USS Raleigh in 1939. The USS *Raleigh* was stationed at Pearl Harbor, Hawaii when the Japanese attacked on December 7, 1941. He fought in the Normandy Invasion known to us as

D-Day. Mr. Thomas Poole was given a Navy Good Conduct Medal and one bar, the American Defense Medal with ribbon and one star, and the American Area Medal with ribbon. He received the European, African, Middle Eastern Area Medal with ribbon and one star; the Asiatic and Pacific Area Medal with ribbon and seven stars; the Philippine Defense Medal with ribbon; and the Victory Medal with ribbon.

History seemed to happen all around Mr. Thomas Poole. He was there when war was declared, and he was in Tokyo serving on the *Oklahoma City* when peace was declared in 1945. He finished out his years in the Navy as a recruiter, retiring, and then going on to work another 20 years at the Cherry Point Marine Corps Base.

Let us all stand in honor and memory of this true patriot and Godly man whose life was devoted to his God, family, and country.

★ ★ ★

"Anchors Aweigh & My Anchor Holds Medley" piano solo by Eric Sexton

Service by Pastor Bill Wingard, titled "The Godly Man"

"Wish You Were Here" sung by Paul Lindsey

A "Celebration of Life" slideshow, with messages:

To our dearest Mr. Tom,

Thanks for all the wonderful memories. To have been a part of your life has been an awesome journey. Your acceptance of us as your family is more dear to our hearts than words could ever express. Enjoy heaven while we wait to meet again, our God-given dad.

Barbara and Jerry Rowe

My Mr. Tom (AKA Granddad),

Thank you for loving me unconditionally and for all your encouragement.

I miss the times we spent watching sports and boxing and talking about hunting and fishing.

We never got to go turkey hunting together, but maybe I can get one in your memory one day. I know you would be proud.

I love you.

Until we meet again…

      Your buddy,

      Sarah

Mr. Tom,

Thank you for the years of love and friendship, for welcoming us into your home as family, and for hours spent around the kitchen table. It is a privilege to have known you.

With all our love,

Jay and Krystal

Closing remarks and prayer by Pastor Bill Wingard

★ ★ ★

We made one addition to Mr. Tom's program, one he would have enjoyed. On the back of the bulletin, we created a word search about Mr. Tom's life.

After the service, we carried his body to Greenleaf Memorial Cemetery, and laid him down next to Amber. After over a decade apart, reunited again.

In the coming days and weeks and months we found a new normal. Things would never go back to the way they were, they couldn't. We each found ways to handle our grief. This short book was mine.

Jay Eldred

Veterans Day

November 11, 2017

New Bern, North Carolina

Post Script

It's been nearly a year since I wrote this ending. As I finally finish the text of this book, Hurricane Florence has wreaked havoc on the city of New Bern and the entire Carolina coast. Though much of downtown is underwater, Mr. Tom's house on the Trent River has survived with minimal damage.

I think back on the hurricanes we weathered in Mr. Tom's house, and can't help but feel nostalgic for time spent sitting with Mr. Tom at the kitchen table, just listening to his stories. I didn't know then just how privileged I was. I only found out after the fact that he didn't talk much about the war with anyone else. On the other hand, he didn't tell me much about his life between his leaving the service and when I first met him in the 2000s. I suppose there's a kind of trade-off.

These certainly aren't the only stories Mr. Tom had to tell. Often he'd get a faraway look in his eyes, but when asked what he was thinking about, he'd reply "nothing". Other times he'd make a seemingly random comment and then refuse to follow up on it. One night we were eating ham and pineapple pizza, and he remarked "This reminds me of my Hawaiian fiancé."

What?!?

"Oh yes," he replied "we all had them. Luaus at least once a week; it was marvelous." But we never got more out of him about it. Another time he casually mentioned he'd once played donkey polo, and said it was harder than it looked.

In the end, I hope this short book has given you an idea of the man I knew: a man I consider to be one of the greatest human beings I have ever met, let alone have the privilege of calling "friend".

Greenville, South Carolina

September 18, 2018

eahtodan eorlscipe   ond his ellenweorc

duguðum démdon.   Swá hit gedéfe bið

þæt mon his winedryhten   wordum herge·

ferhðum fréoge   þonne hé forð scile

of líchaman   laéded weorðan·

They extolled his heroic exploits

And gave thanks for his greatness; which was the proper thing,

For a man should praise a prince whom he holds dear

And cherish his memory when that moment comes

When he has to be convoyed from his bodily home.

Beowulf

Scrapbook

RMS *Queen Elizabeth* bringing American troops back home
New York Harbor, 1945 (via Library of Congress)

Saipan

aboard

USS TARAWA

Commanding Officer	Executive Officer
Captain	Commander
Alvin I. Malstrom	Robert W. Cooper
U.S. Navy	U.S. Navy

Chaplain
Commander
Fred D. Bennett
U.S.N.

Organist   George French Jr. S1c

LIFE

To the preacher life's a sermon;
To the joker life's a jest;
To the miser, life is money;
To the loafer, life is rest.
To the lawyer, life's a trial;
To the poet, life's a song.
To the doctor, life's a patient
That needs treatment right along.
To the soldier, life's a battle;
To the teacher, life's a school.
Life's a great thing to the thinker,
But a failure to the fool.
Life's a long vacation to
The man who loves his work.
It is a constant effort to
Shun duty to the shirk.
To the faithful earnest worker
Life's a story ever new
Life is what we try to make it,
Brother, what is life to you? Selected

Men desiring to sing in church choir, report to after messhall for opening get together at 1400.

Order of Worship

Prelude

The Call to Worship

Hymn No. 346

"I Love to tell the Story" Fisher

The Invocation and the Lord's Prayer

Responsive Reading No. 38

The Gloria Patri

Hymn No. 534

"Shall We Gather at the River" Lowry

Scripture Reading

St. Luke 11:1-30

Hymn No. 349

"Sweet Hour of Prayer" Bradbury

Morning Prayers

Chaplain: The Lord be with you,

Congregation: And with thy spirit,

Chaplain: Let us pray

O Lord, show thy mercy upon us,

Congregation: And grant us thy salvation,

Chaplain: O God, make clean our hearts within us,

Congregation: And take not thy holy spirit from us,

Prayer and Organ Amen

Baptism and Reception of Members

Communion Hymn No. 236

Break Thou The Bread of Life Sherwin

Holy Communion

Hymn no. 430

Take the Name of Jesus with You Baxter

Benediction

Postlude:

old mission
Capistrano

the Mountain Olimpos

St. Sophia Street in Salonica, Greece

St. Demetrious Church

1200 years old

96 ΑΓΙΟΣ ΔΗΜΗΤΡΙΟΣ · ΘΕΣΣΑΛΟΝΙΚΗ   SAINT DEMETRIUS - THESSALONIKI

This is the part we are now in. [Saint] James was killed in dungeon here under the church. There is as much below as you see on top. Church has been rebuilt, but the cells below are the same. Note marble in foreground. Lots of it over here.

Tom in Hawaii

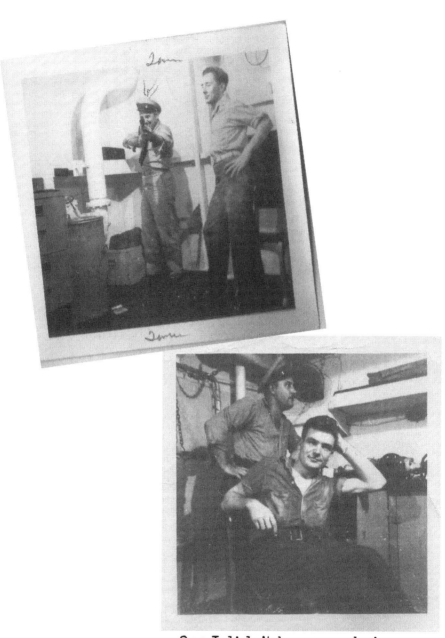

One I didn't know was being taken. The boy is B. Aines.

Drinking "Jo"

Weight – 186

Big, huh! Ha!

You said you like a big man!

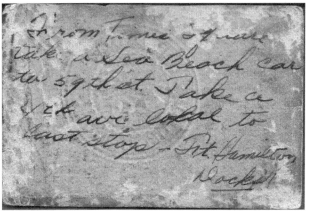

From Times Square take a Sea Beach car to 59th st. Take a 4th ave local to last stops − Ft. Hamilton

BY DIRECT WIRE FROM

WESTERN
UNION

CLASS OF SERVICE		SYMBOLS
This is a full-rate Telegram or Cable-gram unless its deferred character is indicated by a suitable symbol above or preceding the address.		DL = Day Letter
		NL = Night Letter
		LC = Deferred Cable
		NLT = Cable Night Letter
		Ship Radiogram

A. N. WILLIAMS — PRESIDENT   NEWCOMB CARLTON — CHAIRMAN OF THE BOARD   J. C. WILLEVER — FIRST VICE-PRESIDENT

OPK 1 & 2   14   San Francisco, Cal.   11:30 P.   Nov. 17, 1943

Mrs. P. J. Poole
350 Campostella Road
Campostella

Darling, flying across.   Expect to arrive at airport Friday 19th at 9:30
A. M.   Love.

                                   Tom

U.S.S. MEREDITH
LAUNCHED 21 DEC, 1943
BATH IRON WORKS

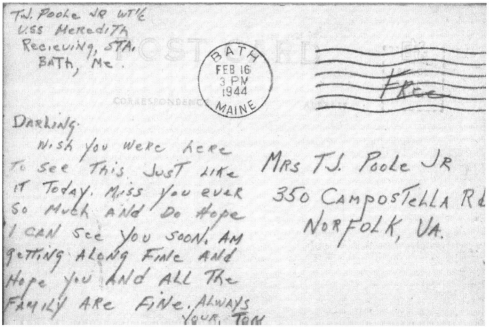

T.J. Poole JR WT1/c
USS Meredith
Recieving, STA.
Bath, Me.

BATH
FEB 16
3 PM
1944
MAINE

Free

Darling,
 Wish you were here to see this. Just like it today. Miss you ever so much and do hope I can see you soon. Am getting along fine and hope you and all the family are fine. Always
 Your, Tom

Mrs T.J. Poole JR
350 Campostehla Rd
Norfolk, Va.

Bridgeton
High School

This Certifies That

Thomas Judson Poole, Jr.

has completed the Course of Study prescribed by the Board of Education for the

Craven County Schools

and is therefore entitled to this Diploma. Given under our hands at Bridgeton this 29th day of May, 1952

Tom & Amber

1947

My Mr America

Me in Alameda Calif.

1942

Me in Norfolk, Va.

Hunting, Trapping, & Fishing

MAKE PATTERN OF PAPER TO FIT TRAP.
& THEN CUT OUT CLOTH.
OLD PANTS OF DENIM WORKS FINE

3" OPENING

MAKE TWO & SEW TOGETHER

PULL TOGETHER & TIE TO SIDE OF TRAP

HOG RING
OR SEW
IN FORWARDS

NYLON
STRING
PULL OPENING
TIGHT

3 or 4"

NYLON
STRING

TIE   30 or 4"   TIE

BAIT IN
THIS SECTION

DOOR OVER   CUT OUT

RUBBER
STRAP

RICKY - THIS IS THE BEST I CAN DO
AS ARTHRITIS IS SO BAD.
ANY QUESTIONS - GIVE ME A CALL.

To Hall + ?

I Know Two Fellows,
   Down on Their Luck.
Chasing Deer Tracks, Hoping
   For A Buck.
They Have Crossed Every
   Road, Field, + Dale
So Far Their Luck Has
   Seemed To Fail.

Built Stands From one
   End of County, To The
   other
Hunted Half Asleep, Starved
   And Tired, Brother. (over)

Now I Asked You Friend
What a Man Lack's,
That'll Spend Half His
Life in The cold, Looking
Dear Tracks?

Signed
"Still ALooking"

Mr. Tom and Barbara

Mr. Tom at the Tryon Palace Pearl Harbor Remembrance Service

December 11, 2016

Photo courtesy Tryon Palace, New Bern, North Carolina

```
R V B V T C V F I F N
Y E O V O R R Q F A A
T N H R E I A G H T M
T Q E T E T M M R H S
I H U N A M E O S E T
W U D A L F V R V R R
E L C N U I D Y A C O
T O M Y V M V N H N P
Z R S R S W S Q A X S
O D U D D T B A Y R M
U S I B R O T H E R G
```

BROTHER   **SPORTSMAN**
FATHER   **SURVIVOR**
FRIEND   **TOM**
GRANDFATHER   **UNCLE**
HERO   **VETERAN**
SMART   **WITTY**

Acknowledgments

I am grateful first and foremost for Mr. Tom; without his friendship this book would not exist. I was also fortunate enough to receive his kitchen table; it was there I hand-wrote the first draft of this book.

Barbara Rowe helped sort through Mr. Tom's papers and photographs and gave my rough draft the highest praise I could ask for:

"It's like he's sitting right here beside me telling the stories all over again."

Amber Sue (Malish) Sconyers and Teresa (Liverman) Etwaroo provided a wealth of information regarding Mr. Tom's family life and the years he told me little about.

Ricky Dupree kindly sent a copy of a letter Mr. Tom mailed him regarding turtling and how to best build a turtle trap.

Leroy and Julia Eldred graciously opened their home to Krystal and me for nearly two weeks during Hurricane Florence, during which the main text of the first draft was completed and formatted.

Unbeknownst to them, Victoria Reynolds Farmer, Michial Farmer, and Kristen Filipic encouraged me to continue writing when I wasn't sure I could do so.

As first readers, Cindy & Carter Williams, Jordan Poss, and Danny Anderson gave valuable insight regarding the finished look, feel, and language of the book.

Our beloved cat Smokey nearly saw this book to completion, passing away September 6, 2018 at the ripe old age of 18. My friend, companion, and sometime editor, he provided much-needed comfort as I once again mourned the loss of Mr. Tom.

Finally, I must thank my wife Krystal for her patience and understanding over the last several years as I rode waves of focused obsession and willful procrastination until finally releasing this work into the wild.

About the Authors

JAY ELDRED is a native of Honesdale, Pennsylvania, but has called the Carolinas home since 2004. He currently resides in New Bern, North Carolina with his wife Krystal, where he teaches history and enjoys reading and running.

THOMAS J. POOLE spent his entire life in Eastern North Carolina, apart from his years in the Navy. He enjoyed the great outdoors and many years of marriage to his sweetheart, Amber. The kind of person to whom history seemed to happen, Tom passed away in 2017.

Made in the USA
Columbia, SC
04 June 2019